5-Ingredients or Less Keto Crock Pot Cookbook

21 Day for Rapid Weight Loss and Burn Fat Forever- Lose up to 20 Pounds in 3 Weeks

Susan Fisch

Table of contents

CHAPTER 1: UNDERSTANDING THE KETO DIET

The History of keto Diet:

Keto diet is a technique developed by modern physicians in the 1920's for treatment of epilepsy; this is one of the most effective treatments for childhood. The keto diet is a high-fat diet with a moderate level of protein and low in carbohydrate in medicine used to treat epilepsy in children. The ketogenic diet forces the human body to burn fats instead of carbohydrates. Keto diet therapy was developed as an alternative option for nonmainstream fasting. Doctors notice that some epilepsy patients have exhibited signs of starving and some patients have low blood sugar. Fasting is using in the treatment of disease has known to human beings for thousands of years ago. Ancient Greek physician studied this in detail, how a man has cured epilepsy when he is enjoying food and drinks. In 1911 the first scientific study of fasting is used as a treatment for epilepsy in France. The experiment was conducted on twenty epilepsy patients all are detox by consuming low-calorie vegetarian.

The process of ketosis

When we eat any types of foods our body processing these foods and various types of nutrients into the different forms of energy such as proteins, carbohydrates, and fats. These are converted into the form of fuel using different metabolic processes. When your body absorbs the excess amount of protein and a high amount of carbohydrates your body breaks it down into the form of glucose. When glucose provides cells with the quickest source of adenosine and three phosphates (ATP), which is the primary source of energy used by the human body. When your body consumes calories from proteins, fats and carbohydrates these calories increase the adenosine and three phosphates (ATP) levels in your body.

Your body stores this energy in two ways:

- Glycogenesis: When glucose level increases in your body excess glucose are converted into the form of glycogen and these glycogens are stored into the muscles and liver. Depending on your health if you do not consume other calories within 7 to 24 hours gap, your body automatically used these glycogens as an alternate energy source
- Lipogenesis: when there is enough number of glycogens are present in your liver and muscles the extra glucose in your body is converted into the form of fats and these facts are stored in your body this process of storing fats are called as lipogenesis. Glycogens are store in our body into limited form, but fats have no limits for storage. These facts are sustaining our body for months without sufficient foods.

In the unexpected situations when glucose and glycogens are insufficient to provide energy in your body, the fats are still used as a fuel in this process the alternate fuel source is producing called as ketones.

When our body does not access any type of foods or you are fasting, sleeping or you have followed a ketogenic diet plan at this stage your body will break down some fats into energy molecules. These energy molecules are called ketones. Our brain uses sugar as a primary source of fuel so that the brain is much more dependent on secondary energy source from ketones.

Reaching ketosis

1. Intake healthy Fats:

   When you consume plenty of healthy fats in daily food. This helps you to boost your ketone level and help you to reach ketosis. Ketogenic diet provides 60 to 70% of calories from fat which is effective for weight loss

   Healthy fats include butter, coconut oil, olive oil, tallow, and lard. There are many healthy fat foods are available which are low in carb and high in fats.

   If your main goal is weight loss then you must very careful about calories, do not consume too many calories in total.

2. Reduce carb consumption:

   The most important is to take very low carb in diet, which is

   helpful for reaching ketosis. Normally your body cells use glucose as the main fuel source. Some of the cells are used as a secondary source such as fatty acids and ketone which is known as ketone bodies.

   Your body stores excess glucose in the form of glycogen and the glycogen are stored in the liver and muscles. When you reduce carb intake glycogen store also reduced, the level of hormone insulin decreases. This results in the fatty acid releases from fat stores in your body and your liver converts into ketones.

3. Use coconut oil in diet:

   Eating coconut oil in your diet may help you to get into

Ketosis because coconut oil contains fats called as medium chain triglycerides (MCT). These facts are rapidly absorbed by the liver directly and immediately converted into ketones.

Consuming coconut oil increases the level of ketones, so it is recommended in some cases like nervous system disorders, Alzheimer disease and it also reduces digestive side effects.

4. Increase your physical activities:

When you are doing physical activity or exercise your body used

glycogen as a fuel. When you take low carb intake automatically glycogen level is low in your body which is helpful to increase production of ketones. These ketones are used as an alternate source of fuel for your muscles. When you are working out in fasted state ketones levels are increased.

5. Adequate Protein Intake:

Adequate protein intake is necessary for achieving ketosis. To

increase ketones production most of the people cutting protein intake which is not a healthy practice. Protein is necessary to supply with amino acid to the liver for making a new glucose in the body.

When you are doing weight loss diet proteins are a most important role to maintain muscle mass with low carb intake. Too little amount of protein intake leads to muscle mass loss whereas the excessive amount of protein intake defeat ketones production. So adequate Protein is necessary for ketosis.

Benefits of the Ketogenic diet

1. **Weight Loss:**

    Low carb diet is one of the effective ways to lose weight.

    Studies on low carb diet show that you can lose weight faster than compared to a low-fat diet. In a low carb diet, you can lose weight 3 times faster than a low-fat diet without being hungry.

2. **Kills your Appetite:**

    Low carb diet is one of the best diets which helps automatic

    reduction in appetite. The studies show that when people cut carbs and eat more fat and proteins which leads to eating much fewer calories.

3. **Abdominal Fat loss:**

    Low carb diet tends to play an important role to reduce

    abdominal fats a large percentage of harmful fats in the abdominal cavity which causes metabolic problems.

4. **Increase the level of HDL in your body:**

    HDL stands for High-Density Lipoprotein which is also

    known as good cholesterol. A higher level of HDL tends to lower the risk of heart disease. Compare to low-fat diet HDL level increase faster in low carb diet.

5. **Reduce blood pressure:**

Blood pressure is one of the important risk factors for many

diseases. Low carb diet is very helpful to reduce blood pressure which reduces the risk of many common diseases.

6. Improve Pattern of LDL:

LDL stands for Low-Density Lipoprotein which is also known

as bad cholesterol. If the LDL level increases in bloodstream risk of heart attack increase usually small particles in the bloodstream have increased the risk of heart disease while large particles have a lower risk.

Low carb diet increases the small LDL particles into large in the bloodstream which are helpful to reduce the risk of heart diseases.

7. Fatty Liver Disease:

The ketogenic diet can very helpful in Non-alcoholic fatty liver disease. Studies done has shown that six month of low carb ketogenic diet leads to weight loss and also an improvement in fatty liver disease.

8. Lower Blood Sugar:

Ketones allow to control and reduce blood sugar levels. It

has the ability to utilize ketones and fat as a fuel, pre-diabetic or type 2 diabetic patients have no longer needed an insulin. Ketogenic diet helps to reduce the excess blood sugar levels.

9. Alzheimer's:

Alzheimer is considered as a type 3 diabetes in which brain

are unable to utilize glucose researcher study shows that significant clinical improvements are observed in Alzheimer patients who have taken the ketogenic diet.

10. Acne:

The ketogenic diet reduces acne in some cases. There are

various causes of acne, one of related to blood sugar and diet. In a diet, processed carb can alter gut bacteria which causes blood sugar fluctuations which can affect skin health.

Keto diet side effects

Ketosis diet is mostly considered as a safe diet plan, but it may lead to some of the side effects. These side effects at beginning a ketogenic diet.

1. Low blood sugar:

   When you are a beginner of ketosis diet low blood sugar is the

   Common ketosis side effect. When your intake more carbs your body putting a certain amount of insulin out to control the sugar. Intake of sugar is reduced on a keto diet.

2. Constipation:

   When you are new to take keto diet you might initially

   experience some constipation. The remedy for constipation is to increase intake of fiber, getting enough salt and eating non-starchy vegetables. If this does not work then cutting dairy products and nuts.

3. Smelly Breath:

   Some peoples face the smelly breath problem, smell of

   acetone on their breath because of eating low carb food. Acetone is one of the ketone bodies created during ketosis. If you have smelly breath problem during keto diet, it takes 2 weeks to adopt ketosis.

4. Heart palpitations:

   During keto diet, you notice that your heart rate increases

slightly this happens only those who have low blood pressure. This will cause because of the lack of water and salt causes a reduction in fluids circulating in the blood, due to this heart to pump slightly faster.

5. Heart and Kidney damage:

   During keto diet, your body can be low on fluid and

   electrolytes increase urination. Due to this body dehydrates this will seriously affect on kidney such as kidney injury, kidney stones. Electrolytes are necessary for normal heartbeats. Some people face irregular heartbeats due to low electrolytes.

Useful Tips and Tricks for a successful keto diet

- Stay Hydrated: Day today's busy lifestyle we forgot to drink plenty of water needed for our body with the result of this we forgot to hydrate effectively. I will recommend hydrate your body by drinking plenty of water. You find this is easier and you will carve the extra hydration.

- Consume enough good salts: When we are on low carb ketogenic diet our kidney excretes more sodium from our body due to lower insulin level to adding additional sodium please follow following tips:
  - Drinking organic broth once a day
  - Use a generous amount of pink salt in daily food
  - Eat sea vegetables like dulse, kelp, nori etc.

- Decrease stress: If you are going through high stress in your life and want to start ketogenic diet may not be the best idea. If you definitely want to start a ketogenic diet you need to reduce your stress in your life to taking enough sleep, exercising regularly adopting meditation technique.

- Consume carbs from vegetable source: You need to consume all necessary nutrients including fibers from the following non- starchy vegetables like broccoli, kale, cabbage, spinach and Brussel sprouts etc. These vegetables are low in calories too.

- Count your carbs: When your aim is weight loss then you should measure daily intake of carbohydrates. Some foods have hidden carb you should know such foods
  - Moist fruits such as blueberry.
  - Chicken wings loaded with buffalo sauce or barbecue.
  - Breaded meats.
  - Milk and low-fat foods like yogurts.

- Cleaning out carbs from your kitchen: You should be cleaning out all pantry from the kitchen of all carbohydrates includes pasta, bread, candy, rice and sodas this will help you to stick to your ketogenic diet.

- Do not eat too much protein: If you eat too much protein your body converts excess proteins in amino acids to glucose. To know how much proteins, you need daily then you should measure your weight and divide your weight by 2.2 to figure out the gram of protein per kg of body weight

- Use MCT Oils: Whenever possible always use MCT oils. MCT oils are made up of coconut oil so it contains capric and caprylic acids that are also called as triglycerides. You can add MCT oils in protein shakes, coffee, tea and green drinks too which helps to keep your ketone level up throughout the day.

CHAPTER2: THE BASIC OF SLOW COOKER

What is the slow cooker

A slow cooker is also known as a crock-pot, is an electrical cooking appliance used for cooking food and simmer at lower heat.

The slow cooker is used to cook mainly for fresh ingredients at low temperature for long period of time.

It also prevents bacteria growth. A microbiologist has tasted slow cooker and found that the heat 200 degrees F maintained for 2 hours or better above the safety limits.

Slow cookers are generally a budget-friendly way to prepare food. Under 400 calories slow cooker meal equal weight loss success.

It helps to lose weight while still enjoying the flavorful meal.

The slow cooker is convenient for batch cooking healthy meals that can last up to 4-5 days.

The best part of the slow cooker is time management you don't need to have to be there for the cook. It cooks for you while you are away and turns off itself when the food is ready.

Using slow cooker, you reduce consumptions of processed foods which will help to reduce the intake of sodium, calories, and fat in your diet.

In many recipes, extended cooking times allow better distribution of flavors.

A slow cooker meal is an excellent choice for a busy day or out of your home.

The slow cooker doesn't need to add oil for cooking this is give you healthier results and better taste.

Benefits of slow cooker

- The slow cooker is better for cooking cheaper cuts like pork shoulder, chicken thighs, lamb shoulder and beef brisket.
- Slow cooker helps to makes meat soften and tender, fall off the bone meat.
- It is one of the healthiest ways to cook meat. When we cook the meat over high heat, the fats and protein in the meat interact with harmful compounds.
- The slow cooker is also used to cook dried beans. You just need to add some water and beans in slow cooker and on it forgot it for 8 to 9 hours. Using this we can avoid canned beans.
- Slow cooker brings out flavors in foods and you can cook a wide variety of foods. Veggies prepared in *slow cookers* can deliver disease-fighting *nutrients*.
- Complimentary spices and herbs are best to add near the end of cooking. In addition, thickeners such as corn starch, and tomato paste uses to give the texture of the dish.
- Ingredients can be taken directly from the refrigerator and placed in a slow cooker it will cause to extend cooking times. If using frozen beef add at least 1 cup of warm liquid to the cooker prior to adding the beef to help prevent sudden temperature changes.
- Vegetables cooked in a slow cooker can absorb spices and stock giving the fuller flavors.

Taking care of your slow cooker

- Thaw frozen poultry and meat in the refrigerator before cooking in the slow cooker. Do not put frozen meat in slow cooker.

- Vegetables are cook slower in slow cooker compare to meat and poultry. Place the vegetables first and second put the meat over it and last is top with broth, sauce or water in slow cooker

- Always put your slow cooker on high for the first hour then turn the setting high to low until finish cooking.

- To prevent curdling add cheese, cream and milk during the last hour

- Soft vegetables such as zucchini, tomatoes, and mushrooms are added when 45 minutes of cooking remaining

- Fill the slow cooker not less than half full and not more than 2/3 full. Too much and too little food in slow cooker affects cooking safety, cooking time and cooking quality.

- For easily clean slow cooker use spray or oil, spray slow cooker inside with nonstick cooking spray.

Comparing slow cooker with other cooking methods

- Time: When pressure cooker cooks food in 50 minutes slow cooker takes 8 hours to cook food
- Texture: Carrots cooks in a pressure cooker comes out mushy and soft whereas slow cooker maintains their shape and texture even bordering being too crisp
- Taste: Gravy cooked near about 8 hours in the slow cooker is richer and tastier than gravy made in a pressure cooker
- Verdict: While the pressure cooker food gives superior tasting but it all depends upon how you want to spend time. Whereas slow cooker has hands-off cooking you just prepare food into the slow cooker, set timing and forgot it. The slow cooker will cook for you.

CHAPTER 3: FOOD TO EAT

- Grass-fed and wild animal meat:

Grass-fed meat such as goat, lamb, beef, seafood and wild caught fish. Eat high in Omega 3 fatty acid from pastured eggs, butter, gelatin, pastured poultry and pork

Eat grass-fed organs meat such as liver, kidneys, and hearts.

- Healthy Fats:

Add some healthy fats in daily diet plan such fats and their sources given as below

- Saturated fats: These fats are found in goose fat, duck fat, coconut oil, butter, tallow, chicken fat and lard
- Polyunsaturated fats: These fats are found from animal sources such as seafood and fatty fish it contains Omega 3 fatty acids.
- Monounsaturated fats: mainly get this fat from olive oil, avocado oil, and macadamia oil
- Fruits and non-starchy vegetables:
  - Fruits: Avocado is the only fruits suitable in keto diet
  - Non-Starchy Vegetables:

Green and leafy vegetables such as spinach, chard, endive, bok choy, radicchio, lettuce.

Also use cruciferous vegetables like radishes, kohlrabi, kale etc.

Cucumber, asparagus, bamboo shoots, celery stalk are used in ketogenic diet meal.

- Condiments and beverages:
  - Black or herbal tea, black coffee, cream coffee, water.

- Fermented foods such as kombucha, kimchi, and sauerkraut, mayonnaise, pesto, bone broth, mustard, pickles.
- All herbs and spices are used such as lime juice and zest

- Eat Occasionally
  - Fruits vegetables and mushroom:
  - Cruciferous vegetables such as all cabbages, broccoli, cauliflower, fennel, Brussel sprouts etc.
  - Sea vegetables such as sugar snap peas, French artichokes, okra, bean sprouts, wax beans
  - Root vegetables such as onion, mushrooms, pumpkin, leek, and garlic
  - Berries such as blue barriers, blackberries, cranberries, strawberries, raspberries, mulberries etc.

- Full Fat Dairy products:
  - Dairy products such as cottage cheese, full-fat yogurt, sour cream, heavy cream etc

- Nuts and seeds:
  - Pine nuts, pumpkin seeds, walnut, pecans, sunflower seeds, sesame seeds, hemp seeds, almonds
  - Macadamia nuts are high in monosaturated fats and it has a very low carb

- Fermented soy products:
  - Eat fermented soy products such as tamari, natto, tempeh
  - Unprocessed green and black soybeans

- Alcohol:
  - Unsweetened spirits, dry white wine, and dry red wine.

CHAPTER 4: FOOD TO AVOID

- Processed Food: Avoid processed food that contains carrageen a such as sulfites gelatin and dried fruits, MSG find in some whey protein products, wheat gluten etc.

- All grains: whole grains such as oats, wheat, millet, sprouted grains, rice, buckwheat, millet, bulgur, sorghum

- All products made from grains such as pizza, cookies, pasta, crackers, bread etc. sweets and sugar such as agave syrup, cakes, ice cream soft drinks and sweet puddings.

- Artificial sweeteners: Avoid artificial sweeteners because they cause carving which produce some health issues such as migraines such as Splenda, equal and sweeteners which contains Aspartame, sucralose, acesulfame etc.

- Food with added sugar: Avoid sweeteners which raise your blood sugar, cause insulin spikes

- Refined oils: Canola, cottonseeds, soybean, sunflower, safflower, corn, grape seed oils

- Tropical fruits: Such as mango, banana, pineapple, papaya, etc. avoid some high carb fruits like grapes, tangerine. Also avoid fresh fruits juices dried fruits like raisins, dates.

- Legumes: Legumes are high in the carb so avoid legumes. It is also hard to digest due to it contains phytates and lectins.

- Avoid soy products: Avoid soy products except for a few non-GMO fermented products which has health benefits and also avoid wheat gluten and use BPA free packaging.

- Milk: Milk is not easily digested. Less number of good bacteria are present in milk. You may take a small amount of raw milk.

- Alcoholic, sweet drinks: Beer, cocktails, sweet wine etc. You can consume low carb drinks and cocktails

CHAPTER 5: TIPs

1. Only consumes keto food and ingredients

2. Track your daily calories intake

3. Plan your meals ahead of times

4. Avoid convenient food

5. Eat those foods that you measure and track

6. Use the meal plan which helps you keep track of your calories

7. Always meal preparation for the week

8. Make your drinks keto friendly

9. While following the keto diet pair a workout to it

10. Consume good fats which provide omega 3

11. Drink lots of water if you follow weight loss

12. To make your favorite meal use low carb ingredients

13. Avoid sugar carving using herbs

14. Keep your energy up with juice and teas

15. Always eat healthy fats

16. Don't over consume protein

17. You have to moderate your protein intake

18. Do not compromise your food quality

CHAPTER 6: FQAs

Where can I find low carb keto recipes?

- Everywhere on the internet. You can find low carb recipes on health and nutrition websites.

How should I track my carb intake?

- There is a various way to measure carb intake. One of most common is mobile fitness app that helps to keep track.

Can I eat too much fat?

- Eating too much fat will push over calories deficit and convert it into a calorie.

Can I drink alcohol during the diet?

- Yes, alcohol can consume during a diet but be careful about hidden carb in the drink.

How long does it take to get ketosis?

- If you are in your optimal carb limit usually it will take 2-3 days to enter ketosis.

Can I eat nuts?

- You can eat nuts but in moderation. Nuts are suitable for ketogenic diet.

Can I eat fruits?

- Yes, you can eat avocados fruit and coconut. You can also eat a moderate amount of low carb fruits such as berries.

Is ketogenic diet suitable for kids?

- Yes, ketosis diet is widely used to cure diseases like autism and epilepsy in kids.

CHAPTER 7: BREAKFAST
Egg Sausage Breakfast Casserole

Preparation Time: 10 minutes

Cooking Time: 4 hours

Serve: 6

Ingredients:

- 4 cups broccoli, chopped
- 10 eggs
- 1 cup cheddar cheese, shredded
- 12 oz sausage, cooked and sliced
- ¾ cup whipping cream
- Pepper and salt

Directions:

- Spray slow cooker from inside with cooking spray.
- Add half broccoli florets to the slow cooker and spread well.
- Add ½ sausages and ½ cheeses into the slow cooker.
- Repeat same with remaining broccoli florets, sausage, and cheese.
- In a bowl, whisk together eggs, pepper, whipping cream, and salt. Pour into the slow cooker.
- Cover slow cooker with lid and cook on low for 4 hours.
- Serve warm and enjoy.

Nutritional Value (Amount per Serving):

- Calories 437
- Fat 34.5 g
- Carbohydrates 5.3 g
- Sugar 1.7 g
- Protein 27 g

- Cholesterol 357 mg

Vegetable Omelet

Preparation Time: 10 minutes

Cooking Time: 1 hour 30 minutes

Serve: 4

Ingredients:

- 6 eggs
- 1 bell pepper, diced
- 1 cup spinach
- ½ cup unsweetened almond milk
- 4 egg whites
- Pepper and salt

Directions:

- Spray slow cooker from inside with cooking spray.
- In a large bowl, whisk together egg whites, eggs, almond milk, pepper, and salt. Stir in bell pepper and spinach.
- Transfer egg mixture to the slow cooker.
- Cover slow cooker with lid and cook on high for 1 hour 30 minutes.
- Slice and serve.

Nutritional Value (Amount per Serving):

- Calories 128
- Fat 7.2 g
- Carbohydrates 3.5 g
- Sugar 2.3 g
- Protein 12.5 g
- Cholesterol 246 mg

Cheese Bacon Quiche

Preparation Time: 10 minutes

Cooking Time: 4 hours

Serve: 8

Ingredients:

- 10 eggs, beaten
- 10 bacon pieces, cooked and chopped
- 8 oz cheddar cheese, shredded
- 1 cup half and half
- ½ cup spinach, chopped
- Pepper and salt

Directions:

- Spray slow cooker from inside with cooking spray.
- In a bowl, whisk together eggs, spinach, cheese, half and half, pepper, and salt.
- Pour egg mixture into the slow cooker. Sprinkle bacon on top.
- Cover slow cooker with lid and cook on low for 4 hours.
- Slice and serve.

Nutritional Value (Amount per Serving):

- Calories 252
- Fat 20.2 g
- Carbohydrates 2.6 g
- Sugar 0.6 g
- Protein 15.6 g
- Cholesterol 246 mg

Egg Breakfast Casserole

Preparation Time: 10 minutes

Cooking Time: 1 hour 30 minutes

Serve: 4

Ingredients:

- 6 eggs
- 1 cup cheese, shredded
- 1 lb ham, chopped into cubes
- 2 green onions, chopped
- ½ cup heavy cream
- Pepper and salt

Directions:

- Spray slow cooker from inside with cooking spray.
- In a bowl, whisk together eggs and heavy cream. Add green onions and ham to the bowl and stir well.
- Pour egg mixture into the slow cooker. Add cheese and black pepper. Stir to mix.
- Cover slow cooker with lid and cook on high for 1 hour.
- Stir well and cook for 30 minutes more.
- Serve warm and enjoy.

Nutritional Value (Amount per Serving):

- Calories 447
- Fat 31.2 g
- Carbohydrates 6.2 g
- Sugar 0.9 g
- Protein 34.6 g
- Cholesterol 360 mg

Cauliflower Breakfast Casserole

Preparation Time: 10 minutes

Cooking Time: 6 hours

Serve: 8

Ingredients:

- 12 eggs
- 1 cauliflower head, shredded
- ½ cup almond milk
- 1 lb sausage, cooked and crumbled
- 2 cups cheddar cheese, shredded
- Pepper and salt

Directions:

- Spray slow cooker from inside with cooking spray.
- In a bowl, whisk together eggs, almond milk, pepper, and salt.
- Add about 3rd shredded cauliflower into the bottom of the slow cooker. Season with pepper and salt.
- Top with about 3rd sausage and 3rd cheese. Repeat the same layers 2 more times.
- Pour egg mixture into the slow cooker.
- Cover slow cooker with lid and cook on low for 6 hours.
- Serve warm and enjoy.

Nutritional Value (Amount per Serving):

- Calories 443
- Fat 35.6 g
- Carbohydrates 3.5 g
- Sugar 2 g
- Protein 27.4 g

Veggie Frittata

Preparation Time: 10 minutes

Cooking Time: 4 hours

Serve: 4

Ingredients:

- 6 eggs
- 2 tsp Italian seasoning
- 1/4 cup cherry tomatoes, sliced
- 4 oz mushrooms, sliced
- ½ cup cheese, shredded
- Pepper and salt

Directions:

- Spray slow cooker from inside with cooking spray.
- Spray medium pan with cooking spray and heat over medium heat.
- Add mushrooms and cherry tomatoes to the pan and cook until softened.
- Transfer vegetables to the slow cooker.
- In a bowl, whisk together eggs, cheese, pepper, and salt.
- Pour egg mixture into the slow cooker.
- Cover slow cooker with lid and cook on low for 4 hours.
- Slice and serve.

Nutritional Value (Amount per Serving):

- Calories 167
- Fat 12 g
- Carbohydrates 2.3 g
- Sugar 1.6 g
- Protein 12.8 g
- Cholesterol 262 mg

Feta Spinach Quiche

Preparation Time: 10 minutes

Cooking Time: 8 hours

Serve: 6

Ingredients:

- 8 eggs
- ¾ cup feta cheese, crumbled
- ¾ cup parmesan cheese, shredded
- 2 cups spinach, chopped
- 2 cups unsweetened coconut milk
- Pepper and salt

Directions:

- Spray slow cooker from inside with cooking spray.
- In a bowl, whisk together eggs and coconut milk.
- Add spinach, parmesan cheese, feta cheese, and salt and stir to combine.
- Pour egg mixture into the slow cooker.
- Cover slow cooker with lid and cook on low for 8 hours.
- Slice and serve.

Nutritional Value (Amount per Serving):

- Calories 375
- Fat 32.6 g
- Carbohydrates 6.5 g
- Sugar 3.9 g
- Protein 17.2 g
- Cholesterol 245 mg

Cauliflower Mashed

Preparation Time: 10 minutes

Cooking Time: 6 hours

Serve: 4

Ingredients:

- 1 medium cauliflower head, cut into florets
- 2 garlic cloves, minced
- 1 ½ cups water
- Pepper and salt

Directions:

- Add cauliflower florets, garlic, and water into the slow cooker.
- Cover slow cooker with lid and cook on low for 6 hours.
- Drain cauliflower well and transfer into the large bowl.
- Mash cauliflower using the potato masher until smooth and creamy.
- Season with pepper and salt.
- Stir well and serve warm.

Nutritional Value (Amount per Serving):

- Calories 38
- Fat 0.2 g
- Carbohydrates 8.1 g
- Sugar 3.5 g
- Protein 3 g
- Cholesterol 0 mg

CHAPTER 8: APPITIZER & SNACKS

Spicy Pecans

Preparation Time: 10 minutes

Cooking Time: 3 hours

Serve: 16

Ingredients:

- 3 lbs pecan halves
- 2 tbsp Cajun seasoning blend
- 2 tbsp olive oil

Directions:

- Add all ingredients to the slow cooker and stir well to combine.
- Cover slow cooker with lid and cook on low for 1 hour.
- Stir well. Cover again and cook for 2 hours more.
- Serve and enjoy.

Nutritional Value (Amount per Serving):

- Calories 607
- Fat 62.5 g
- Carbohydrates 12.2 g
- Sugar 3 g
- Protein 9.1 g
- Cholesterol 0 mg

Tasty Seasoned Mixed Nuts

Preparation Time: 10 minutes

Cooking Time: 2 hours

Serve: 20

Ingredients:

- 8 cups mixed nuts
- 3 tbsp curry powder
- 4 tbsp butter, melted
- Salt

Directions:

- Add all ingredients into the slow cooker and stir well to combine.
- Cover slow cooker with lid and cook o high for a ½ hour. Stir again and cook for 30 minutes more.
- Cover again and cook on low for 1 hour more.
- Stir well and serve.

Nutritional Value (Amount per Serving):

- Calories 375
- Fat 34.7 g
- Carbohydrates 12.8 g
- Sugar 2.5 g
- Protein 9 g
- Cholesterol 6 mg

Nacho Cheese Dip

Preparation Time: 10 minutes

Cooking Time: 2 hours

Serve: 8

Ingredients:

- 8 oz cream cheese, cut into chunks
- ¼ cup almond milk
- ½ cup chunky salsa
- 1 cup cheddar cheese, shredded

Directions:

- Add all ingredients to the slow cooker and stir well.
- Cover slow cooker with lid and cook on low for 2 hours. Stir to mix.
- Serve with fresh vegetables.

Nutritional Value (Amount per Serving):

- Calories 178
- Fat 16.4 g
- Carbohydrates 2.4 g
- Sugar 0.9 g
- Protein 6.1 g
- Cholesterol 46 mg

Easy Texas Dip

Preparation Time: 10 minutes

Cooking Time: 6 hours

Serve: 8

Ingredients:

- 1 ½ cups Velveeta cheese, cubed
- 2 cups fresh tomatoes, diced
- 4 oz can green chilies, diced
- 1 large onion, chopped

Directions:

- Add all ingredients into the slow cooker and stir well to combine.
- Cover slow cooker with lid and cook on low for 6 hours.
- Stir well and serve.

Nutritional Value (Amount per Serving):

- Calories 104
- Fat 7.2 g
- Carbohydrates 4.4 g
- Sugar 2.1 g
- Protein 6 g
- Cholesterol 22 mg

Cheese Chicken Dip

Preparation Time: 10 minutes

Cooking Time: 2 hours

Serve: 10

Ingredients:

- ½ cup bell peppers, chopped
- 1 cup chicken breast, cooked and shredded
- 12 oz can tomato with green chilies
- ½ lb cheese, cubed

Directions:

- Add all ingredients into the slow cooker and stir well to combine.
- Cover slow cooker with lid and cook on low for 2 hours.
- Stir well and serve.

Nutritional Value (Amount per Serving):

- Calories 120
- Fat 8 g
- Carbohydrates 2 g
- Sugar 0.4 g
- Protein 10 g

Flavorful Mexican Cheese Dip

Preparation Time: 10 minutes

Cooking Time: 1 hour

Serve: 6

Ingredients:

- 1 tsp taco seasoning
- ¾ cup tomatoes with green chilies
- 8 oz Velveeta cheese, cut into cube

Directions:

- Add cheese into the slow cooker. Cover and cook on low for 30 minutes. Stir occasionally.
- Add taco seasoning and tomatoes with green chilies and stir well.
- Cover again and cook on low for 30 minutes more.
- Stir well and serve.

Nutritional Value (Amount per Serving):

- Calories 159
- Fat 12.6 g
- Carbohydrates 1.9 g
- Sugar 0.3 g
- Protein 9.6 g

Salsa Beef Dip

Preparation Time: 10 minutes

Cooking Time: 1 hour

Serve: 20

Ingredients:

- 32 oz salsa
- 2 lbs Velveeta cheese, cubed
- 2 lbs ground beef

Directions:

- Brown beef in a pan over medium heat. Drain well and transfer to the slow cooker.
- Add cheese and salsa and stir well.
- Cover slow cooker with lid and cook on high for 1 hour.
- Stir well and serve.

Nutritional Value (Amount per Serving):

- Calories 279
- Fat 17.9 g
- Carbohydrates 3.4 g
- Sugar 1.6 g
- Protein 25.8 g
- Cholesterol 88 mg

Chapter 9: BEEF, LAMB & PORK

Kalua Pork with Cabbage

Preparation Time: 10 minutes

Cooking Time: 9 hours

Serve: 12

Ingredients:

- 1 medium cabbage head, chopped
- 3 lbs pork shoulder butt roast, trimmed
- 7 bacon slices
- 1 tbsp sea salt

Directions:

- Place 4 bacon slices into the bottom of slow cooker.
- Spread pork roast on top of bacon slices and season with salt.
- Arrange remaining bacon slices on top of pork roast layer.
- Cover slow cooker with lid and cook on low for 8 hours or until meat is tender.
- Add chopped cabbage. Cover again and cook on low for 1 hour.
- Remove pork from slow cooker and shred using a fork.
- Return shredded pork to the slow cooker and stir well.
- Serve warm and enjoy.

Nutritional Value (Amount per Serving):

- Calories 264
- Fat 18.4 g
- Carbohydrates 4.4 g
- Sugar 2.4 g
- Protein 20.5 g
- Cholesterol 71 mg

Creamy Pork Chops

Preparation Time: 10 minutes

Cooking Time: 6 hours

Serve: 4

Ingredients:

- 4 boneless pork chops
- ½ cup chicken stock
- 1 oz dry ranch dressing
- 10.5 oz chicken soup
- 3 garlic cloves, minced
- Pepper

Directions:

- Season pork chops with pepper and place in slow cooker.
- In a bowl, mix together chicken soup, ranch dressing, stock, and garlic.
- Pour chicken soup mixture over top of pork chops.
- Cover slow cooker with lid and cook on low for 6 hours.
- Serve hot and enjoy.

Nutritional Value (Amount per Serving):

- Calories 280
- Fat 15.1 g
- Carbohydrates 7.4 g
- Sugar 1 g
- Protein 29.1 g
- Cholesterol 64 mg

Beef Taco Filling

Preparation Time: 10 minutes

Cooking Time: 6 hours

Serve: 12

Ingredients:

- 1 lb ground beef
- 10 oz can tomato with green chilies
- 1 envelope taco seasoning

Directions:

- Add all ingredients to the slow cooker and stir well.
- Cover slow cooker with lid and cook on low for 6 hours.
- Serve and enjoy.

Nutritional Value (Amount per Serving):

- Calories 75
- Fat 2.4 g
- Carbohydrates 0.9 g
- Sugar 0.6 g
- Protein 11.7 g
- Cholesterol 34 mg

Flavorful Steak Fajitas

Preparation Time: 10 minutes

Cooking Time: 6 hours

Serve: 6

Ingredients:

- 2 lbs beef, sliced
- 2 tbsp fajita seasoning
- 20 oz salsa
- 1 large onion, sliced
- 1 bell pepper, sliced

Directions:

- Add salsa into the slow cooker.
- Add remaining ingredients on top of salsa and stir to mix.
- Cover slow cooker with lid and cook on low for 6 hours.
- Stir well and serve.

Nutritional Value (Amount per Serving):

- Calories 333
- Fat 9.7 g
- Carbohydrates 11.9 g
- Sugar 5 g
- Protein 47.8 g
- Cholesterol 135 mg

Garlic Herb Pork

Preparation Time: 10 minutes

Cooking Time: 8 hours

Serve: 10

Ingredients:

- 3 lbs pork shoulder roast, boneless and cut into 4 pieces
- ½ tbsp cumin
- ½ tbsp fresh oregano
- 2/3 cup grapefruit juice
- 6 garlic cloves
- Pepper and salt

Directions:

- Add pork roast into the slow cooker. Season with pepper and salt.
- Add garlic, cumin, oregano, and grapefruit juice into the blender and blend until smooth.
- Pour blended mixture over pork and stir well.
- Cover slow cooker with lid and cook on low for 8 hours.
- Remove pork from slow cooker and shred using a fork.
- Return shredded pork into the slow cooker and stir well.
- Serve warm and enjoy.

Nutritional Value (Amount per Serving):

- Calories 359
- Fat 27.8 g
- Carbohydrates 2.1 g
- Sugar 1.1 g
- Protein 23.2 g

Garlic Thyme Lamb Chops

Preparation Time: 10 minutes

Cooking Time: 6 hours

Serve: 8

Ingredients:

- 8 lamb chops
- 1 tsp dried oregano
- 2 garlic cloves, minced
- ½ tsp dried thyme
- 1 medium onion, sliced
- Pepper and salt

Directions:

- Add sliced onion into the slow cooker.
- Combine together thyme, oregano, pepper, and salt. Rub over lamb chops.
- Place lamb chops in slow cooker and top with garlic.
- Pour ¼ cup water around the lamb chops.
- Cover slow cooker with lid and cook on low for 6 hours.
- Serve and enjoy.

Nutritional Value (Amount per Serving):

- Calories 40
- Fat 1.9 g
- Carbohydrates 2.3 g
- Sugar 0.6 g
- Protein 3.4 g
- Cholesterol 0 mg

Pork Tenderloin

Preparation Time: 10 minutes

Cooking Time: 4 hours

Serve: 6

Ingredients:

- 1 ½ lbs pork tenderloin, trimmed and cut in half lengthwise
- 6 garlic cloves, chopped
- 1 oz envelope dry onion soup mix
- ¾ cup red wine
- 1 cup water
- Pepper and salt

Directions:

- Place pork tenderloin into the slow cooker.
- Pour red wine and water over pork.
- Sprinkle dry onion soup mix on top of pork tenderloin.
- Top with chopped garlic and season with pepper and salt.
- Cover slow cooker with lid and cook on low for 4 hours.
- Stir well and serve.

Nutritional Value (Amount per Serving):

- Calories 196
- Fat 4 g
- Carbohydrates 3.1 g
- Sugar 0.9 g
- Protein 29.9 g
- Cholesterol 83 mg

Smoky Pork with Cabbage

Preparation Time: 10 minutes

Cooking Time: 8 hours

Serve: 6

Ingredients:

- 3 lbs pastured pork roast
- 1/3 cup liquid smoke
- 1/2 cabbage head, chopped
- 1 cup water
- 1 tbsp kosher salt

Directions:

- Rub pork with kosher salt and place into the slow cooker.
- Pour liquid smoke over the pork. Add water.
- Cover slow cooker with lid and cook on low for 7 hours.
- Remove pork from slow cooker and add cabbage in the bottom of slow cooker.
- Now place pork on top of the cabbage.
- Cover again and cook for 1 hour more.
- Shred pork with a fork and serve.

Nutritional Value (Amount per Serving):

- Calories 484
- Fat 21.5 g
- Carbohydrates 3.5 g
- Sugar 1.9 g
- Protein 65.4 g
- Cholesterol 195 mg

Simple Roasted Pork Shoulder

Preparation Time: 10 minutes

Cooking Time: 9 hours

Serve: 8

Ingredients:

- 4 lbs pork shoulder
- 1 tsp garlic powder
- 1/2 cup water
- 1/2 tsp black pepper
- 1/2 tsp sea salt

Directions:

- Season pork with garlic powder, pepper, and salt and place in slow cooker. Add water.
- Cover slow cooker with lid and cook on high for 1 hour then turn heat to low and cook for 8 hours.
- Remove meat from slow cooker and shred using a fork.
- Serve and enjoy.

Nutritional Value (Amount per Serving):

- Calories 664
- Fat 48.5 g
- Carbohydrates 0.3 g
- Sugar 0.1 g
- Protein 52.9 g
- Cholesterol 204 mg

Flavors Pork Chops

Preparation Time: 10 minutes

Cooking Time: 4 hours

Serve: 4

Ingredients:

- 4 pork chops
- 2 garlic cloves, minced
- 1 cup chicken broth
- 1 tbsp poultry seasoning
- 1/4 cup olive oil
- Pepper and salt

Directions:

- In a bowl, whisk together olive oil, poultry seasoning, garlic, broth, pepper, and salt.
- Pour olive oil mixture into the slow cooker then place pork chops into the slow cooker.
- Cover slow cooker with lid and cook on high for 4 hours.
- Serve and enjoy.

Nutritional Value (Amount per Serving):

- Calories 386
- Fat 32.9 g
- Carbohydrates 2.9 g
- Sugar 0.7 g
- Protein 19.7 g

Beef Stroganoff

Preparation Time: 10 minutes

Cooking Time: 8 hours

Serve: 2

Ingredients:

- 1/2 lb beef stew meat
- 1/2 cup sour cream
- 2.5 oz mushrooms, sliced
- 10 oz mushroom soup
- 1 medium onion, chopped
- Pepper and salt

Directions:

- Add all ingredients except sour cream into the slow cooker and mix well.
- Cover slow cooker with lid and cook on low for 8 hours.
- Add sour cream and stir well.
- Serve and enjoy.

Nutritional Value (Amount per Serving):

- Calories 471
- Fat 25.3 g
- Carbohydrates 8.6 g
- Sugar 3.1 g
- Protein 48.9 g
- Cholesterol 109 mg

Chili Lime Beef

Preparation Time: 10 minutes

Cooking Time: 6 hours

Serve: 4

Ingredients:

- 1 lb beef chuck roast
- 1 tsp chili powder
- 2 cups lemon-lime soda
- 1 fresh lime juice
- 1 garlic clove, crushed
- 1/2 tsp salt

Directions:

- Place beef chuck roast into the slow cooker.
- Season roast with garlic, chili powder, and salt.
- Pour lemon-lime soda over the roast.
- Cover slow cooker with lid and cook on low for 6 hours. Shred the meat using a fork.
- Add lime juice over shredded roast and serve.

Nutritional Value (Amount per Serving):

- Calories 355
- Fat 16.8 g
- Carbohydrates 14 g
- Sugar 11.3 g
- Protein 35.5 g
- Cholesterol 120 mg

CHAPTER 10: POULTRY & CHICKEN

Moist Turkey Breast

Preparation Time: 10 minutes

Cooking Time: 4 hours

Serve: 12

Ingredients:

- 6 lbs turkey breast, bone-in
- ½ cup water
- 4 garlic cloves, peeled
- 4 fresh rosemary sprigs
- Pepper and salt

Directions:

- Place turkey breast into the slow cooker.
- Add water, garlic, and rosemary on top. Season with pepper and salt.
- Cover slow cooker with lid and cook on low for 4 hours or until meat is tender.
- Serve and enjoy.

Nutritional Value (Amount per Serving):

- Calories 237
- Fat 3.8 g
- Carbohydrates 9.9 g
- Sugar 8 g
- Protein 38.8 g
- Cholesterol 98 mg

Simple Shredded Turkey

Preparation Time: 10 minutes

Cooking Time: 7 hours

Serve: 24

Ingredients:

- 4 lbs turkey breast, skinless, boneless, and halves
- 1 envelope onion soup mix
- ½ cup butter, cubed
- 12 oz chicken stock

Directions:

- Place turkey breast into the slow cooker.
- Combine together butter, chicken stock, and onion soup mix and pour over turkey breast.
- Cover slow cooker with lid and cook on low for 8 hours.
- Shred turkey breast with a fork and serve.

Nutritional Value (Amount per Serving):

- Calories 113
- Fat 5.1 g
- Carbohydrates 3.2 g
- Sugar 2.7 g
- Protein 13 g
- Cholesterol 43 mg

3-Delicious Salsa Verde Chicken

Preparation Time: 10 minutes

Cooking Time: 4 hours

Serve: 4

Ingredients:

- 4 chicken breasts, skinless and boneless
- ½ cup cilantro, chopped
- 1 ½ cups Monterey jack cheese, shredded
- 16 oz salsa

Directions:

- Spray slow cooker from inside with cooking spray.
- Place chicken breasts into the slow cooker then pour salsa over the chicken.
- Cover slow cooker with lid and cook on low for 4 hours.
- Before 30 minutes of serving sprinkle cheese on top of chicken.
- Garnish with cilantro and serve.

Nutritional Value (Amount per Serving):

- Calories 467
- Fat 23.8 g
- Carbohydrates 7.5 g
- Sugar 3.7 g
- Protein 54.4 g
- Cholesterol 168 mg

Tasty Salsa Chicken

Preparation Time: 10 minutes

Cooking Time: 2 hours

Serve: 6

Ingredients:

- 1 ½ lbs chicken tenders, skinless
- 16 oz salsa
- 1/8 tsp ground cumin
- 1/8 tsp oregano
- ¼ tsp garlic powder

Directions:

- Place chicken tenders into the slow cooker. Season with cumin, oregano, and garlic powder.
- Pour salsa over the chicken tenders.
- Cover slow cooker with lid and cook on high for 2 hours.
- Remove chicken from slow cooker and shred with a fork.
- Return shredded chicken to the slow cooker and stir well.
- Serve and enjoy.

Nutritional Value (Amount per Serving):

- Calories 237
- Fat 8.5 g
- Carbohydrates 4.9 g
- Sugar 2.3 g
- Protein 34 g
- Cholesterol 101 mg

Delicious Harissa Chicken

Preparation Time: 10 minutes

Cooking Time: 4 hours

Serve: 4

Ingredients:

- 1 lb chicken breasts, skinless and boneless
- 1 cup harissa sauce
- ¼ tsp garlic powder
- ½ tsp ground cumin
- ½ tsp kosher salt

Directions:

- Season chicken with cumin, kosher salt, and garlic powder.
- Place chicken to the slow cooker.
- Pour harissa sauce over the chicken.
- Cover slow cooker with lid and cook on low for 4 hours.
- Remove chicken breasts from slow cooker and shred using a fork.
- Return shredded chicken to the slow cooker and stir well.
- Serve and enjoy.

Nutritional Value (Amount per Serving):

- Calories 232
- Fat 9.7 g
- Carbohydrates 1.3 g
- Sugar 0.1 g
- Protein 32.9 g

Tomatillo Chicken Drumsticks

Preparation Time: 10 minutes

Cooking Time: 6 hours

Serve: 6

Ingredients:

- 6 chicken drumsticks, bone-in, and skin removed
- 1 tsp olive oil
- 1 tsp dried oregano
- 1 tbsp apple cider vinegar
- 1 ½ cups tomatillo sauce
- Pepper and salt

Directions:

- Add all ingredients into the slow cooker and stir well to combine.
- Cover slow cooker with lid and cook on low for 6 hours.
- Serve and enjoy.

Nutritional Value (Amount per Serving):

- Calories 106
- Fat 3.9 g
- Carbohydrates 3.2 g
- Sugar 1 g
- Protein 13.7 g
- Cholesterol 40 mg

CHAPTER 11: FISH & SEAFOOD

Cilantro Lime Salmon

Preparation Time: 10 minutes

Cooking Time: 2 hours

Serve: 4

Ingredients:

- 1 lb salmon fillets
- 3 tbsp fresh lime juice
- 2 garlic cloves, chopped
- 3/4 cup fresh cilantro, chopped
- 1 tbsp olive oil
- Pepper and salt

Directions:

- Add olive oil into the slow cooker then place salmon fillets to the slow cooker.
- In a small bowl, combine together lime juice, garlic, cilantro, and olive oil.
- Pour bowl mixture over the salmon.
- Cover slow cooker with lid and cook on low for 2 hours.
- Serve and enjoy.

Nutritional Value (Amount per Serving):

- Calories 228
- Fat 13.5 g
- Carbohydrates 1.4 g
- Sugar 0.2 g
- Protein 24.1 g
- Cholesterol 70 mg

Lemon Tilapia

Preparation Time: 10 minutes

Cooking Time: 2 hours

Serve: 4

Ingredients:

- 4 tilapia fillets
- 12 asparagus spears
- 2 tbsp butter, divided
- 1/4 tsp lemon pepper seasoning
- 10 tbsp fresh lemon juice

Directions:

- Take four foil pieces.
- Place each fish fillet on each foil piece.
- Sprinkle lemon pepper seasoning and lemon juice on top of fish fillet.
- Add 1/2 tablespoon of butter on top of each fillet.
- Arrange three asparagus spears on each fish fillet. Fold foil over the fillet and seal the ends.
- Repeat same with remaining fish fillets.
- Place fish fillet packet into the slow cooker and cook on high for 2 hours.
- Serve and enjoy.

Nutritional Value (Amount per Serving):

- Calories 110
- Fat 6.7 g
- Carbohydrates 3.7 g
- Sugar 2.2 g
- Protein 10 g
- Cholesterol 37 mg

Paprika Shrimp

Preparation Time: 10 minutes

Cooking Time: 50 minutes

Serve: 8

Ingredients:

- 2 lbs raw shrimp, peeled and deveined
- 1 tsp paprika
- 6 garlic cloves, sliced
- 1/4 tsp red pepper flakes
- 3/4 cup olive oil
- Pepper and salt

Directions:

- Combine together oil, red pepper flakes, black pepper, paprika, garlic, and salt into the slow cooker.
- Cover and cook on high for 30 minutes. Add shrimp and stir well.
- Cover and cook on high for 10 minutes.
- Stir well and cover again and cook for 10 minutes more.
- Serve warm and enjoy.

Nutritional Value (Amount per Serving):

- Calories 301
- Fat 20 g
- Carbohydrates 2.7 g
- Sugar 0.1 g
- Protein 26 g
- Cholesterol 239 mg

Capers Rosemary Salmon

Preparation Time: 10 minutes

Cooking Time: 2 hours

Serve: 2

Ingredients:

- 8 oz salmon
- 2 tbsp lemon juice
- 1/4 tsp fresh rosemary, minced
- 1 tbsp capers
- 1/3 cup water

Directions:

- Place salmon into the slow cooker.
- Pour lemon juice and water over salmon.
- Sprinkle with rosemary and capers.
- Cover slow cooker with lid and cook on low for 2 hours.
- Serve and enjoy.

Nutritional Value (Amount per Serving):

- Calories 164
- Fat 7.3 g
- Carbohydrates 3.3 g
- Sugar 1.1 g
- Protein 22.6 g
- Cholesterol 50 mg

Shrimp Soup

Preparation Time: 10 minutes

Cooking Time: 2 hours 10 minutes

Serve: 4

Ingredients:

- 2 tbsp fajita seasoning
- 1 onion, sliced
- 1 bell pepper, sliced
- 64 oz chicken stock
- 1 lb shrimp

Directions:

- Add all ingredients except shrimp to the slow cooker and stir well.
- Cover slow cooker with lid and cook on high for 2 hours.
- Add shrimp and cook for 10 minutes more.
- Stir well and serve.

Nutritional Value (Amount per Serving):

- Calories 189
- Fat 3.1 g
- Carbohydrates 11.1 g
- Sugar 4 g
- Protein 27.7 g

Coconut Shrimp Curry

Preparation Time: 10 minutes

Cooking Time: 2 hours

Serve: 4

Ingredients:

- 1 lb shrimp
- 2 1/2 tsp lemon garlic seasoning
- 1 tbsp curry paste
- 30 oz unsweetened coconut milk
- 15 oz water

Directions:

- Add all ingredients except shrimp to the slow cooker and stir well.
- Cover slow cooker with lid and cook on high for 2 hours.
- Add shrimp and cook for 15 minutes more.
- Stir well and serve.

Nutritional Value (Amount per Serving):

- Calories 200
- Fat 7.7 g
- Carbohydrates 4.6 g
- Sugar 0 g
- Protein 26 g
- Cholesterol 239 mg

Shrimp Scampi

Preparation Time: 10 minutes

Cooking Time: 1 hours 30 minutes

Serve: 6

Ingredients:

- 1 1/2 lbs shrimp
- 2 tbsp lemon juice
- 4 garlic cloves, minced
- 6 tbsp olive oil
- 1 1/2 cup chicken broth
- Pepper and salt

Directions:

- Add all ingredients to the slow cooker and stir well to combine.
- Cover slow cooker with lid and cook on high for 1 hour 30 minutes.
- Stir well and serve.

Nutritional Value (Amount per Serving):

- Calories 269
- Fat 16.3 g
- Carbohydrates 2.7 g
- Sugar 0.3 g
- Protein 27.2 g
- Cholesterol 239 mg

CHAPTER 12: VEGAN

Flavorful Italian Mushrooms

Preparation Time: 10 minutes

Cooking Time: 4 hours

Serve: 6

Ingredients:

- 1 lb mushrooms
- 1 envelope Italian dressing mix
- ½ cup butter, melted
- 1 large onion, sliced

Directions:

- Add onion and mushrooms to the slow cooker and mix well.
- Combine together butter and Italian dressing mix and pour over onion and mushroom.
- Cover slow cooker with lid and cook on low for 4 hours.
- Serve and enjoy.

Nutritional Value (Amount per Serving):

- Calories 162
- Fat 15.6 g
- Carbohydrates 4.8 g
- Sugar 2.4 g
- Protein 2.8 g
- Cholesterol 41 mg

Vegetable Fajitas

Preparation Time: 10 minutes

Cooking Time: 3 hours 30 minutes

Serve: 4

Ingredients:

- 1 cup cherry tomatoes, halved
- 1 tsp smoked paprika
- 1 tbsp olive oil
- 3 bell peppers, cut into strips
- 1 onion, sliced
- Pepper and salt

Directions:

- Add onion, bell peppers, oil, smoked paprika, pepper, and salt into the slow cooker and stir well.
- Cover slow cooker with lid and cook on high for 1 1/2 hours.
- Add cherry tomatoes and cook for another 2 hours.
- Stir well and serve.

Nutritional Value (Amount per Serving):

- Calories 79
- Fat 3.9 g
- Carbohydrates 11.4 g
- Sugar 6.9 g
- Protein 1.7 g
- Cholesterol 0 mg

Root Vegetables

Preparation Time: 10 minutes

Cooking Time: 2 hours 30 minutes

Serve: 3

Ingredients:

- 3/4 lb mixed root vegetables
- 2 garlic cloves, peeled
- 1/2 onion, sliced
- 1/8 tsp salt

Directions:

- Add all ingredients to the slow cooker and mix well.
- Cover slow cooker with lid and cook on high for 2 1/2 hours.
- Serve and enjoy.

Nutritional Value (Amount per Serving):

- Calories 59
- Fat 0.4 g
- Carbohydrates 11.1 g
- Sugar 5.6 g
- Protein 0.3 g
- Cholesterol 0 mg

Healthy Brussels sprouts

Preparation Time: 10 minutes

Cooking Time: 2 hours

Serve: 8

Ingredients:

- 2 lbs Brussels sprouts
- 3 tbsp dried cranberries
- 2 tbsp olive oil
- Pepper and salt

Directions:

- Add all ingredients to the slow cooker and stir well.
- Cover and cook on low for 2 hours.
- Stir well and serve immediately.

Nutritional Value (Amount per Serving):

- Calories 80
- Fat 3.9 g
- Carbohydrates 10.5 g
- Sugar 2.5 g
- Protein 3.9 g
- Cholesterol 0 mg

Roasted Broccoli

Preparation Time: 10 minutes

Cooking Time: 2 hours

Serve: 4

Ingredients:

- 2 lbs broccoli florets
- 2 tsp olive oil
- 1 bell pepper, chopped
- Pepper and salt

Directions:

- Add all ingredients to the slow cooker and stir well to mix.
- Cover slow cooker with lid and cook on high for 2 hours.
- Stir well and serve.

Nutritional Value (Amount per Serving):

- Calories 89
- Fat 3.2 g
- Carbohydrates 13.3 g
- Sugar 0.7 g
- Protein 7 g

Super Easy Carrots

Preparation Time: 10 minutes

Cooking Time: 3 hours

Serve: 8

Ingredients:

- 2 lbs carrots, peeled and sliced
- ¼ cup coconut oil, melted
- 1/8 tsp nutmeg
- ¼ tsp cinnamon
- ¼ cup coconut sugar
- Pepper and salt

Directions:

- Add all ingredients to the slow cooker and stir well to combine.
- Cover and cook on high for 3 hours.
- Stir well and serve immediately.

Nutritional Value (Amount per Serving):

- Calories 98
- Fat 5.8 g
- Carbohydrates 11.2 g
- Sugar 5.6 g
- Protein 1 g
- Cholesterol 15 mg

Roasted Whole Cauliflower

Preparation Time: 10 minutes

Cooking Time: 6 hours

Serve: 6

Ingredients:

- 1 medium cauliflower head, green removed and trimmed and cut the bottom
- 2 tbsp ranch dressing
- 1 cup vegetable stock
- 1 tbsp ranch salad dressing and seasoning mix

Directions:

- Place cauliflower into the slow cooker.
- Rub both the seasoning over the cauliflower and pour stock in the bottom of the slow cooker.
- Cover slow cooker with lid and cook on low for 6 hours.
- Place cauliflower on a baking tray and broil for 3-4 minutes.
- Cut into wedges and serve.

Nutritional Value (Amount per Serving):

- Calories 32
- Fat 0.5 g
- Carbohydrates 6.7 g
- Sugar 2.8 g
- Protein 2 g
- Cholesterol 0 mg

CHAPTER 13: SOUPS & STEW

Curried Cauliflower Soup

Preparation Time: 10 minutes

Cooking Time: 6 hours

Serve: 2

Ingredients:

- 1/2 lb cauliflower florets
- 1 garlic clove, minced
- 1/2 onion, minced
- 1 1/2 tsp curry powder
- 1 1/4 cup water

Directions:

- Add all ingredients to the slow cooker and stir well.
- Cover slow cooker with lid and cook on low for 6 hours.
- Puree the soup using an immersion blender until smooth.
- Serve and enjoy.

Nutritional Value (Amount per Serving):

- Calories 46
- Fat 0.4 g
- Carbohydrates 10 g
- Sugar 4 g
- Protein 2.8 g
- Cholesterol 0 mg

Creamy Pumpkin Soup

Preparation Time: 10 minutes

Cooking Time: 4 hours

Serve: 6

Ingredients:

- 30 oz can pumpkin puree
- 5 cups vegetable stock
- 2 garlic cloves, minced
- 1 medium onion, diced
- 1/4 tsp dried thyme
- Pepper and salt

Directions:

- Add pumpkin puree, vegetable stock, thyme, garlic, and onion into the slow cooker. Stir well.
- Cover slow cooker with lid and cook on low for 4 hours.
- Puree the soup using a blender until smooth and creamy. Season with pepper and salt.
- Stir well and serve.

Nutritional Value (Amount per Serving):

- Calories 57
- Fat 0.9 g
- Carbohydrates 12.9 g
- Sugar 5.8 g
- Protein 2.6 g
- Cholesterol 0 mg

Creamy Broccoli Soup

Preparation Time: 10 minutes

Cooking Time: 4 hours 30 minutes

Serve: 4

Ingredients:

- 12 oz broccoli florets
- 1 cup heavy cream
- 4 cups chicken stock
- 1 small onion, diced
- Pepper and salt

Directions:

- Add broccoli, chicken broth, onion, pepper, and salt to the slow cooker and stir well.
- Cover slow cooker with lid and cook on low for 4 hours.
- Puree the soup using an immersion blender until smooth and creamy.
- Stir in heavy cream. Cover again and cook on low for 30 minutes.
- Stir well and serve.

Nutritional Value (Amount per Serving):

- Calories 149
- Fat 12 g
- Carbohydrates 8.9 g
- Sugar 2.9 g
- Protein 3.9 g
- Cholesterol 41 mg

Delicious Mushroom Soup

Preparation Time: 10 minutes

Cooking Time: 4 hours 30 minutes

Serve: 4

Ingredients:

- 8 oz mushrooms, washed and sliced
- 1 cup heavy cream
- 4 cups chicken broth
- 1 small onion, diced
- Pepper and salt

Directions:

- Add mushrooms, chicken broth, onion, pepper, and salt to the slow cooker.
- Cover slow cooker with lid and cook on low for 4 hours.
- Puree the soup using a blender until smooth and creamy.
- Stir in heavy cream. Cover again and cook for 30 minutes more.
- Stir well and serve.

Nutritional Value (Amount per Serving):

- Calories 161
- Fat 12.7 g
- Carbohydrates 5.2 g
- Sugar 2.4 g
- Protein 7.4 g
- Cholesterol 41 mg

Cheesy Cauliflower Soup

Preparation Time: 10 minutes

Cooking Time: 4 hours 30 minutes

Serve: 6

Ingredients:

- 12 oz cauliflower, cut into florets
- 1 cup heavy cream
- 1 cup cheddar cheese, grated
- 4 oz cream cheese, cut into cubes
- 5 cups chicken broth
- Pepper and salt

Directions:

- Add cauliflower, chicken broth, onion, pepper, and salt to the slow cooker.
- Cover slow cooker with lid and cook on low for 4 hours.
- Puree the soup using an immersion blender until smooth.
- Stir in cream, cheddar cheese, and cream cheese.
- Cover again and cook for 30 minutes more.
- Stir well and serve.

Nutritional Value (Amount per Serving):

- Calories 139
- Fat 10.2 g
- Carbohydrates 15.1 g
- Sugar 8 g
- Protein 1.7 g

Perfect Pumpkin Soup

Preparation Time: 10 minutes

Cooking Time: 8 hours

Serve: 4

Ingredients:

- 2 cups pumpkin puree
- 1 onion, minced
- ¼ tsp ground nutmeg
- 1 cup unsweetened coconut milk
- 4 cups water

Directions:

- Add all ingredients into the slow cooker and stir well to combine.
- Cover slow cooker with lid and cook on low for 8 hours.
- Puree the soup using an immersion blender until smooth and creamy.
- Stir well and serve hot.

Nutritional Value (Amount per Serving):

- Calories 65
- Fat 1.4 g
- Carbohydrates 13.1 g
- Sugar 5.3 g
- Protein 1.7 g
- Cholesterol 0 mg

Simple Pork Stew

Preparation Time: 10 minutes

Cooking Time: 8 hours

Serve: 4

Ingredients:

- 2 lbs pork stew meat, cubed
- 1 packet onion soup mix
- 2 carrots, peel and slice
- 2 garlic cloves, minced
- 1 ½ cups water
- Pepper and salt

Directions:

- Add all ingredients into the slow cooker and stir well to combine.
- Cover slow cooker with lid and cook on low for 8 hours.
- Stir well and serve.

Nutritional Value (Amount per Serving):

- Calories 501
- Fat 21.9 g
- Carbohydrates 4.7 g
- Sugar 1.6 g
- Protein 66.9 g
- Cholesterol 195 mg

CHAPTER 14: DESSERTS

Applesauce

Preparation Time: 10 minutes

Cooking Time: 2 hours

Serve: 6

Ingredients:

- 3 lbs fresh apples, peel, core, and slice
- 1/4 cup water
- 2 whole cinnamon sticks
- 2 tbsp fresh lemon juice

Directions:

- Add all ingredients to the slow cooker and stir well.
- Cover slow cooker with lid and cook on high for 2 hours.
- Discard cinnamon sticks and using potato masher mash until you get desired consistency.

Nutritional Value (Amount per Serving):

- Calories 59
- Fat 0.2 g
- Carbohydrates 15.5 g
- Sugar 11.7 g
- Protein 0.3 g
- Cholesterol 0 mg

Chocolate Fudge

Preparation Time: 10 minutes

Cooking Time: 2 hours

Serve: 30

Ingredients:

- 2 ½ cups chocolate chips, sugar-free
- 2 tsp liquid stevia
- 1 tsp vanilla extract
- 1/3 cup unsweetened coconut milk

Directions:

- Add stevia, vanilla, chocolate chips, and coconut milk into the slow cooker and stir well.
- Cover slow cooker with lid and cook on low for 2 hours.
- Open the lid and stir until smooth.
- Grease casserole dish with butter and spread mixture into the dish.
- Place dish in the refrigerator for 30 minutes or until fudge firm.
- Cut fudge into the pieces and serve.

Nutritional Value (Amount per Serving):

- Calories 81
- Fat 4.8 g
- Carbohydrates 8.5 g
- Sugar 7.3 g
- Protein 1.1 g
- Cholesterol 3 mg

Almond Chocolate Fudge

Preparation Time: 10 minutes

Cooking Time: 6 hours

Serve: 30

Ingredients:

- 2 tbsp almonds, sliced
- ½ cup unsweetened coconut milk
- 1 tbsp butter, melted
- 2 tbsp stevia
- 8 oz unsweetened chocolate chips

Directions:

- Grease 8" baking dish with butter and set aside.
- Add chocolate chips, coconut milk, butter, and stevia into the slow cooker and mix well.
- Cover slow cooker with lid and cook on low for 2 hours.
- Add almonds and stir fudge until smooth.
- Pour fudge mixture into the baking dish and spread well. Place dish in the refrigerator for 6 hours.
- Cut into squares and serve.

Nutritional Value (Amount per Serving):

- Calories 15
- Fat 1.5 g
- Carbohydrates 0.3 g
- Sugar 0.2 g
- Protein 0.2 g
- Cholesterol 1 mg

Cinnamon Pecans

Preparation Time: 10 minutes

Cooking Time: 3 hours

Serve: 6

Ingredients:

- 3 cups pecans, sliced
- 10 drops liquid stevia
- 1 ½ tsp vanilla extract
- 1 tbsp cinnamon
- ¾ tsp salt

Directions:

- Spray slow cooker from inside with cooking spray.
- Add all ingredients to the slow cooker and stir well.
- Cover slow cooker with lid and cook on low for 2 hours. Stir after 1 hour.
- Transfer pecans mixture onto a baking sheet.
- Allow to cool completely then serve.

Nutritional Value (Amount per Serving):

- Calories 146
- Fat 14.7 g
- Carbohydrates 3.7 g
- Sugar 0.8 g
- Protein 2.1 g
- Cholesterol 0 mg

Cinamon Apples

Preparation Time: 10 minutes

Cooking Time: 3 hours

Serve: 10

Ingredients:

- 9 cups apple, diced
- ½ tsp nutmeg
- 2 tsp ground cinnamon
- 1 ½ cups water
- 2 tbsp fresh lemon juice

Directions:

- Add all ingredients to the slow cooker and stir well.
- Cover slow cooker with lid and cook on high for 3 hours.
- Stir well and serve.

Nutritional Value (Amount per Serving):

- Calories 50
- Fat 0.2 g
- Carbohydrates 13.1 g
- Sugar 10.1 g
- Protein 0.3 g

Delicious Custard

Preparation Time: 10 minutes

Cooking Time: 2 hours

Serve: 6

Ingredients:

- 2 eggs
- 2 egg yolks
- 10 drops liquid stevia
- ½ cup almond milk
- 1 cup heavy cream

Directions:

- Add all ingredients to the blender and blend until well combined.
- Spray ramekins with cooking spray and pour batter into each ramekin.
- Place ramekins into the slow cooker.
- Cover slow cooker with lid and cook on high for 2 hours.
- Serve and enjoy.

Nutritional Value (Amount per Serving):

- Calories 154
- Fat 15.1 g
- Carbohydrates 2 g
- Sugar 0.8 g
- Protein 3.6 g
- Cholesterol 152 mg

Yummy Pumpkin Custard

Preparation Time: 10 minutes

Cooking Time: 5 hours

Serve: 6

Ingredients:

- 3 cups can pumpkin
- 2 tbsp coconut oil
- 10 drops liquid stevia
- ¼ cup coconut milk
- 6 eggs

Directions:

- Pour 1 inch of water into the slow cooker.
- Add all ingredients into the blender and blend until smooth.
- Spray ramekins with cooking spray.
- Pour blended mixture into the prepared ramekins and place into the slow cooker.
- Place ramekins into the slow cooker.
- Cover slow cooker with lid and cook on high for 5 hours.
- Serve warm and enjoy.

Nutritional Value (Amount per Serving):

- Calories 167
- Fat 11.6 g
- Carbohydrates 10.8 g
- Sugar 4.7 g
- Protein 7.1 g
- Cholesterol 164 mg

CONCLUSION

What I like most about the ketogenic diet is how easy it is, both when cooking at home and eating out. The recipes in this book are easy and use familiar foods. I will show you how to turn every day, easy-to-find ingredients into keto-friendly recipes that are delicious and full of the healthy fats your body will use to fuel itself. The most important step in starting a ketogenic diet is just starting! Do not feel intimidated: this book will walk you through everything you need to know!

Made in the USA
Las Vegas, NV
13 April 2024

88663859R00052